GREENHOUSE GARDENING

GREENHOUSE GARDENING

Ethne Clarke

WITH A FOREWORD BY
MAX DAVIDSON

SUNBURST BOOKS

This edition first published in 1996 by
Sunburst Books,
Deacon House,
65 Old Church Street,
London SW3 5BS.

ISBN 1 85778 168 6

Publishing Manager *Casey Horton*
Design Manager *Ming Cheung*
Editor *Jennifer Spaeth*
Designer *Sean Bennett*

Publisher's Note
Readers should note that plant breeders introduce new cultivars all the time.
Please check your seed catalogues for the latest ones.

WARNING
If using chemical herbicides,
fungicides or insecticides, be sure to
follow exactly the manufacturer's
instructions

Printed in Hong Kong

CONTENTS

FOREWORD

Greenhouses greatly widen our ability to garden by allowing us to raise all sorts of plants from seed and to grow those plants which would not succeed outdoors under certain weather conditions. The true essence of a greenhouse is that it enables gardeners living away from subtropical latitudes to control the climate with the changing seasons rather than having to be at the mercy of the vagaries of weather.

At its most basic, without additional heating other than that provided free by the sun, a greenhouse is a valuable aid for seed raising and for providing shelter during the winter for plants which would otherwise be killed by cold and wet conditions.

When properly equipped with heating, adequate ventilation and a means of shading the glass from the sun on the hottest of days, a greenhouse gives us the ability to grow virtually any type of plant from bulbs through alpines and cacti to orchids.

Even in northern latitudes gardeners can grow exotic fruit and vegetables. You can have figs in pots, you can train a vine up under the glass roof or grow a fan peach or nectarine tree against one of the sides.

When choosing a greenhouse, it is best to get the largest one you can afford but one which will still fit in happily with the size of your garden. You will also be able to choose between wood and aluminium. Wood looks pleasing to the eye, but needs much more work to maintain than aluminium, which, with its slimmer glazing bars, has the great advantage of allowing in much more light. But do remember that you get what you pay for. A more substantial aluminium greenhouse with roof, side braces and sturdy glazing bars can sometimes contain four times as much metal as a cheaper greenhouse; the metal can flex in strong winds and cause the glass to break.

Most people become concerned with heating costs, but forget that preventing a greenhouse from becoming too hot in summer is often the greater problem. Few plants are happy in temperatures above 86°F/30°C, and it is very difficult in small greenhouses to maintain a stable temperature without wild fluctuations. Conversely, many plants, even exotics, simply need a frost-free winter environment, which can be achieved with good insulation, thermostatically-controlled heating and, particularly in large greenhouses, by sectioning off a small area where higher temperatures can be maintained.

By using the large selection of modern technology that is available today, you need not be a slave to your greenhouse.

No matter what type of greenhouse you choose, gardening under glass adds one more exciting dimension to the satisfaction of being able to grow plants well.

MAX DAVIDSON

INTRODUCTION

There is nothing new or revolutionary about the idea of growing flower and vegetable crops under glass, either to prolong the growing season or to cultivate plants that are not suited to your climate or soils. Pliny the Elder, the Roman scholar, had a fantastic country villa on a hillside outside Rome. His gardens there were extensive; they were ornamented with topiary, box hedging and glass frames that he positioned over the grape vines, strawberries and roses to ensure that he was able to enjoy these delicacies out of season.

During the early Renaissance period, the Medici rulers of Florence – Cosimo de' Medici and Lorenzo the Magnificent – were both keen gardeners and followed Pliny's example, but instead of portable frames they had permanent houses erected in which to cultivate exotic and rare plants; other glass-fronted houses were also constructed in which the pot-grown lemon and orange trees that decorated the formal gardens of the Italian villas and palazzos were overwintered. Palms and date trees were also grown in these elegant, spacious buildings.

With the discovery and colonisation of the New World, many previously unknown flowers, fruit and vegetables were introduced to the gardens of the Old World. Some caught on immediately, while others only gained acceptance after much trial and error. The tomato was naively regarded by many, at first, as poisonous as they became ill from eating the leaves and fruit of this weird new plant. Pineapples were an immediate success, and wealthy gardeners, in their eagerness to raise the first and best crops, built pineapple houses, which were glass-walled structures with elaborate heating systems and deeply dug hot beds filled with heat-generating layers of composting manure. Thus the science of glasshouse, or greenhouse gardening evolved, reaching its heyday in

the late 18th-early 19th centuries with the construction of vast metal-frame and glass-glazed structures, such as the Palm House at the Royal Botanic Gardens, Kew, London and the equally splendid glasshouse at Chatsworth Hall, Derbyshire, England. Both structures were designed by Sir Joseph Paxton, the pioneer of glasshouse architecture.

Victorian gardeners were no less enthusiastic about the possibilities glasshouses offered, as they were devoted to the art of bedding out, which required masses of tender and exotic annuals to create the intricate formal displays of lurid colour they so loved. In addition, the glasshouse was essential for providing the quantities of fresh fruit and cut flowers needed to sustain the average upper middle class family while in residence at their London house. Generous baskets of peaches, pineapples, violets and orchids were transported by train from country seat to town house, often on a daily basis; special baskets and vases were also made to keep the produce in prime condition during the long journey.

From the working greenhouse came the ornamental conservatory, a highly decorative structure attached to the house in which the most choice plants were cultivated. Smaller conservatories were constructed to fit into windows and there were even tabletop models fashioned after the Wardian cases used by plant hunters to transport specimens collected in the wild back to the botanic gardens.

Greenhouses remained the work-horse buildings upon which much ingenuity was spent devising heating systems, irrigation methods, new and better methods of construction and more durable materials. Twentieth-century gardeners harvest the benefit of the previous generation's inventiveness, and there is now a wide range of styles available to suit every greenhouse gardener's criteria.

TYPES OF GREENHOUSE

SHAPES AND MATERIALS ACCOUNT for the differences between the various types of greenhouse available to today's gardeners. There are standard free-standing 'four walls and a roof' greenhouses; lean-to greenhouses, which are attached to an existing wall; pyramid-shaped greenhouses (to take advantage of the sunlight); A-frame greenhouses, which look rather like the cold frames and hot beds of old-fashioned estate gardens; Dutch greenhouses, which have a shape similar to an airplane hanger and, on the cutting edge of modern design, geodesic domes. Frames are made from a variety of materials including wood, metal or plastic and can be glazed with glass, polyurethane sheeting or polycarbonate sheeting.

Wood-frame, glass-glazed greenhouses are the traditional style and the natural materials ensure that the building blends easily into the garden setting. The best wooden greenhouses are made from western red cedar, which is the most resistant to rot; teak and oak are also used and although fairly tough woods, they lack the long-term durability of cedar. Wood frames should be treated against rot during manufacture, which means you should only have to paint the greenhouse with wood preservative every four or five years – saving time and money.

Wood-frame greenhouses must be erected on a concrete plinth to keep the base from direct contact with the damp soil. Some owners like to erect the wood frame on a low brick foundation, only three or four courses high. This foundation adds to the overall appearance and also to the longevity of the greenhouse.

Interior fittings are easy to install simply by drilling into the wooden battens and frame, and the glass panes are fitted just like a house window using glazing nails and putty. This is because the wood will expand and contract with the weather, so the glass must have some give to accommodate the fluctuations. When a glass pane breaks it can be a nuisance having to scrape out the old putty, but the insulation of a putty-glazed window is marginally better than the clip fittings of a metal-frame house.

The timber frame, because of its large size, which is necessary to support the structure and the glass, will be heavier than the frame of an

ABOVE: Polytunnels, made from polythene sheeting stretched over a tubular frame, are used most often by commercial growers; they are difficult to fit into most domestic garden settings because of their size and appearance.

RIGHT: Wood-frame greenhouses are the most traditional of greenhouses, and the natural material used in their construction makes them suitable for ornamental gardens.

RIGHT: Most aluminium greenhouses come in DIY assembly kits; it is a good idea to enlist the aid of a fellow DIY enthusiast to help construct the frame, since all angles must be true and sides parallel to achieve a good fit with the glass glazing.

aluminium-frame greenhouse; this means that there is less light in a wood-frame greenhouse. This is balanced to some extent by the fact that the wood will retain heat, so it can be a few degrees warmer than metal-frame houses. Also, most heat loss is through the glass, so if the total glazed area is less, the house may be several degrees warmer.

Polytunnels are practical greenhouses most often used by professional nurserymen where practicality is more important than appearances. Inexpensive and easy to erect, they are made from metal alloy tubing covered with polythene sheeting.

You can't use just any polythene sheeting – it must be of sturdy weight and have an ultra-violet (UV) inhibitor. These factors help to prolong its life but, even so, plastic will, in a few years, become brittle and yellow with age, when it must be replaced. Light is an important factor to successful greenhouse gardening and plastic also attracts dust, which cuts down on the amount of light the plants will receive. Long-wave solar radiation is what warms a greenhouse, but plastic does not retain this crucial phenomena so, once the sun sets, the plastic greenhouse will cool rapidly.

Polycarbonate sheeting is constructed of layers of special UV-resistant plastic; the layers are sandwiched together to form channels that act as heat-retaining cells. It admits more light and retains more heat than polythene sheeting. This material can be used with wood or metal frames, is quite resilient to accidental impact and is much more durable than polythene sheeting.

Aluminium-and-glass greenhouses are no doubt the most popular greenhouses for the amateur on the market. They are reasonably priced, durable, maintenance-free and easy to erect for average to skilled DIY enthusiasts. However, don't even think about putting one up yourself if hand-eye coordination is not one of your strong points; suppliers can make it sound so easy, but don't be fooled. The glass is simply fitted into rubber glazing strips or mastic and held with clips. The narrowness of a metal frame admits more light into the greenhouse than a wood frame

LEFT: Aluminium greenhouses are by far the most popular, as they are comparatively inexpensive, low-maintenance and flexible, being able to accommodate all sorts of uses; this greenhouse is fitted out with a sun lounger as well as an array of decorative plants.

LEFT: Lean-to greenhouses put against a sunny wall are a useful feature in small gardens where space is at a premium.

does, but it will also cool rather more quickly since metal conducts heat and cold more actively. You can obtain aluminium greenhouses in a wide range of shapes and sizes. Choose the largest one you can afford since greenhouse gardening, once you get into the expanded horizons of gardening it offers, will soon render most houses too small. I began my greenhouse experience looking at a house 1.8 m x 2.4 m/6 ft x 8 ft, thinking that would be adequate as I didn't want gardening under glass to take over my gardening life. Fortunately, a friend pointed out the error of my logic and I bought a 2.4 m x 3.6 m/8 ft x 12 ft greenhouse. I'm glad I did, but I am beginning to wonder about adding on another section. I could also link two aluminium greenhouses side by side – that would really give me some scope.

Considerations When Building a Greenhouse

Some greenhouses come with integral bases, for others it is recommended that you erect them on a concrete slab. My neighbour has carpeted his greenhouse with industrial-gauge horticultural fabric mulch, while my house is settled comfortably on the hard clay pan at the edge of the courtyard behind the house. The gravel layer spread over the clay has long since been walked in, so it is relatively dry underfoot, and spills and messes disappear readily.

My greenhouse is a standard house shape, four walls and a roof sloping from the central ridge, but there are the alternatives I mentioned earlier. Geodesic domes, Dutch houses, pyramids and circular houses all offer optimum light conditions and are good at transmitting solar heat. Lean-to greenhouses placed against a sunny, south-facing wall will require shading, since the wall will act as a solar storage radiator, absorbing energy and then releasing it throughout the day; shading will prevent the house turning into an oven. Placed against an east or west facing wall, the heat and light levels can be boosted by painting the support wall brilliant white. Other

RIGHT: Greenhouses are available in a wide range of shapes and sizes: the hexagonal house is rather more decorative than a straightforward standard square.

BELOW: Geodesic domes have a sort of future-world appeal.

greenhouses should be positioned in the sunniest part of the garden, with the orientation being east-west to make the most of the winter light, especially if you will be using the house to overwinter ornamental plants; houses used only for raising summer crops can be oriented north-south. Position away from overhanging trees and away from the shadow-fall of houses, outbuildings, hedges and fences. Having said that, if your garden is windswept it is a good idea to locate the greenhouse next to, but not up against, a sheltering hedge. Glasshouses are particularly vulnerable to damage and windchill from strong winds.

Other factors affecting site are irrigation of the house, power points and heating. There are various types of watering systems available, which will be outlined later, but the one thing they all have in common is that they require a source of water. Most water requirements, including drip systems, will be satisfied by a narrow gauge water pipe, but for mist propagation units and some other systems, you will probably need more pressure and volume, so a wide bore pipe of at least 2.5 cm/1 in will be required. All water pipes to the house should be laid at least 60 cm/24 in deep beneath a layer of bricks so that the pipe will not be broken by any future excavations.

Lighting may be necessary, so an electricity supply should be arranged – but be sure to call in an electrician to install the wiring. In a greenhouse you will be working with water in moist conditions and, as water and electricity are a potentially lethal combination, it is important to get the best advice and service available to avoid disaster. Always make a map of the exact locations of underground water pipes and electricity cables and keep it where you can find it.

Those are the options; now consider the following points to help you decide what sort of house you need. Many people use their houses to grow tender-flowering ornamentals, which they bring into their homes for decoration; if this is your plan, choose a wood-frame house for its heat-retaining capabilities. If you are planning to raise tender plants in quantities you must realise that these plants require a bit more heat during the early part of the year. Insulation can help to keep the heating costs

ABOVE: A wood-frame greenhouse with a crop of bedding plants hardening off outside its entrance is the sort of productive scene a greenhouse makes possible.

RIGHT: In the depths of winter, a greenhouse with just enough heat to keep frost at bay allows the gardener to grow an enormous range of tender plants, and to expand the uses of the garden.

down. However, heaters are relatively inexpensive to buy and are also fairly reasonable to run.

Other gardeners want to grow vegetable and fruit crops, such as melons, cucumbers, early lettuce and tomatoes; for this purpose a full-glass, metal-frame house with its good light levels is the choice. But if you want to do a bit of both, then go for the full-glass house because it is the most versatile system.

If you have small children who will be playing close to the house, it is worth considering a plastic version to avoid possible injuries from broken glass. If your pocketbook won't stretch to the size of house you want, make sure the one you purchase is expandable.

Other considerations when deciding the details of your chosen green-house are: make sure the house has ventilation in the form of louvre windows. These windows are found on the sides and ridge vents of the greenhouse and also on the roof, either side of the ridge beam; there should be at least one louvre window on each side of the roof. The combination of wall and roof vents is essential in keeping the air fresh and circulating in order to discourage disease. Does the greenhouse have an integral base or will you be required to pour concrete or lay a horticultural fabric carpet? What sort of staging will you have to invest in? Does it have a gutter which can feed into water butts to collect rainfall? How easy will it be to obtain replacement parts should any be needed?

Shop around, ask gardening friends what they think of their green-houses and visit display gardens to see greenhouses in operation to help you assess your needs. Buying a greenhouse is rather like buying a house, but, fortunately, considerably less expensive and nerve wracking.

RIGHT: Grape vines thrive in the warmth of this aluminium greenhouse.

BELOW: In a walled garden, a greenhouse such as this one, built against a south-facing wall, was a familiar sight; the broad expanse of roof glazing captured plenty of light and heat so these houses were often used to rasie fruit crops.

GREENHOUSE FIXTURES AND FITTINGS

KITTING OUT A GREENHOUSE CAN BE just as absorbing as furnishing a house – you will be spoiled for choice. The primary concern will be selecting the sort of staging you install. Like the greenhouse itself, it can be made of wood or aluminium – I haven't come across any plastic staging yet.

Staging

Staging should be high enough so that you do not have to stoop over to work on the plants; it should be sturdy enough to bear the weight of the trays, pots and so on and adaptable to allow for a change of arrangement or use, if necessary. Wood staging with slat tops is the traditional sort, but it is the nature of wood to deteriorate when perpetually damp, as it would be in a greenhouse. For that reason, aluminium staging is the popular choice of most hobby gardeners. There are so many combinations of bases, tops and sizes that you should be able to get exactly what you want. In my greenhouse I use aluminium tray tops spread with a thin layer of gravel; one section is for propagating, and has deep trays with a soil-heating cable beneath a layer of silver sand; another section is mesh-topped to allow good drainage and free air circulation around the potted plants. This is a highly versatile system and the staging is lightweight and maintenance-free. During the summer, I move half the staging outdoors to allow room in the greenhouse for crops of tomatoes, basil and melons. The outdoor staging then serves as a waiting area for new plants, trays of seedlings and pots of plants hardening off before transplanting.

ABOVE AND RIGHT: Wooden staging with slatted tops is the traditional sort of shelving that is used most often in wood-frame greenhouses, but it does require maintenance.

Temperature Control and Lighting

Just as in the garden, plants in a greenhouse require three things: light, heat and water. The first two are intimately linked; short-wave solar radiation from the sun's rays enters the house through the glass walls, warming everything on which it shines. Pots, staging, wood and metal frames and plants heat up, releasing long-wave radiation. This radiation is

LEFT: An electric fan heater fitted with a thermostatic control provides a clean and efficient source of heat in greenhouses during winter.

unable to pass through the glass, so remains trapped in the greenhouse, creating a warm atmosphere. Therefore, it is essential to keep the glass clean to permit as much light as possible to pass through. A considerable amount of the sun's rays are deflected from upright greenhouse walls; that is why geodesic domes, Dutch houses, A-frames and so on with steeply sloping sides are more heat and light efficient.

Long-wave radiation, however, can be boosted by artificial heating, which is important during short winter days. There are various means of applying artificial heating, such as paraffin oil heaters, piped or bottled gas and electricity.

PIPED AND BOTTLED GAS

This form of heating requires a good deal of installation, which in the case of piped gas must be done by a professional. Bottled gas is somewhat easier to install but should also be done by the supplier. A sheltered place must be found for the gas bottles (you will need two botttles with an automatic changeover device; if one gas bottle runs out while you are asleep, the other will kick in automatically). Portable bottled gas units are a possibility but, if your greenhouse is well-insulated, you may find that as the available oxygen is consumed in combustion, the safety mechanism will extinguish the flame. There can also be quite a bit of condensation generated, which leads to a buildup of algae on glass and frames.

PARAFFIN HEATERS

These heaters are inexpensive to run and the individual units are low-priced, but it is not the cleanest system and wicks must be kept trimmed and flues balanced to avoid a shroud of black smut filling the greenhouse and settling on plants. As with gas heaters, you must provide some ventilation to allow for adequate combustion and to avoid a buildup of harmful fumes and condensation.

BELOW: Metal staging is another clean and efficient method of equipping a greenhouse; it is long lasting and requires no upkeep.

**RIGHT: If you require a
constant high level of heat in
the greenhouse, propane gas is
a good choice, but the tanks
are difficult to accommodate.**

ELECTRIC HEATERS

This is the cleanest system, the easiest to install, the most dependable
source of artificial heat and, if used properly in conjunction with a thermostat and some form of insulation on the glazing during winter, not as
expensive to run as you might suppose. As mentioned earlier, if you have
to have electricity supplied to the greenhouse, have it done professional-
ly. That way you will be confident that the cables are properly insulated,
sockets are waterproof, outlets are adequate to provide the amount of
electricity needed and that there is a mains safety fuse.

ELECTRIC HEATING UNITS

For greenhouses, electric units will be some sort of fan or convector heater that draws in cold air, heats it as it passes over the warming cables and then blows it out again. This avoids a buildup of cold spots, since the air is kept moving around the house, unlike a stationary gas system, which only heats the air around it.

You should buy the heater according to the size of your greenhouse and the degree of heat at which you wish to keep it. Most fan heaters will have a thermostatic setting device; follow the manufacturer's instructions for setting it up. When positioning the heater, remember that the

LEFT: Electric heaters come in a wide range of sizes to fit every type of greenhouse. Be sure to choose one which is adequate for your gardening needs.

ABOVE: **On the brightest days in summer a greenhouse will need shading if it is not to over heat; here roller blinds have been fitted against the roof on the oustide.**

machine will be more efficient if you raise it away from the floor and position it as near as possible to the centre of the house; I simply stand my little fan heater on a stool. This makes certain that the air is kept at an even temperature throughout the house. DO NOT USE DOMESTIC FAN HEATERS – these units are not insulated against the humid conditions that prevail in most greenhouses.

Insulation can help to reduce fuel bills in much the same way as double-glazing cuts down on heat loss from house windows. Some greenhouse manufacturers will provide their own double-glazing system, but the average amateur greenhouse gardener will find that bubble plastic, similar to the sort used for packing, will satisfy their demands. It is available from garden centres and DIY stores, and is measured off the roll so you purchase just what you need.

Bubble plastic is easily fitted to the frames of wood or metal houses using drawing pins, staples or special pegs that slot into the grooves of metal-frame uprights. Remember, don't take the insulation over the vents and windows; do these separately so that they can still be opened. Much heat is lost through the roof, so on really cold nights throw a tarpaulin or an old blanket or tablecloth over the roof for added insulation.

Bubble plastic and most other forms of insulation cut down on the amount of short-wave radiation entering the house, so should be removed in the spring when seed-sowing is the main activity, as seedlings need all the light they can get for healthy growth.

Apart from the vents on the sides and on the roof, you can assist good ventilation by installing an extractor fan; this piece of equipment is especially useful in polytunnels because the levels of condensation are so much greater. If you feel the extractor is rather more than your small greenhouse requires, I recommend using a small portable fan. Either one can be used with a thermostat set to engage the fan when temperatures reach your desired maximum. Fans are also useful during winter, since good air circulation is important in keeping mildew and grey mould disease at bay. This is another advantage of the thermostatically controlled electric fan heater. Because it is always left on, heating only when the thermostat engages the element, the fan is constantly circulating the air.

Thermostats will be built-in features of many of the fittings you buy for the greenhouse, but it is a good idea to have a thermostat that registers the maximum high and low. That way you can keep track of how cold it is getting in the greenhouse – and adjust the heating if necessary – or how hot it becomes – and decide if you need to use shading to cut down on the solar heat that is generated.

The most frequently used sort of shading is paint on the exterior; shading paints are specially made for the purpose, resisting the heaviest downpour but easily wiped off the glass with a cloth. Other methods of shading involve rollerblinds fitted either externally or internally. If you're

ABOVE: Cucumber plants climb by means of twisting tendrils.

ABOVE: A piece of netting is attached inside to part of the glazing to protect the plants that do not require full sun.

not too concerned about appearances, you can use a tarpaulin or even an old blanket to throw over the greenhouse if the heat becomes too much. But that is only a temporary measure; if you need shading frequently, invest in a proper system.

Apart from these necessities, there are a few other mechanical gadgets you may want to install to help you run an efficient greenhouse. Lighting can be useful if you live in a short-season area; many gardeners will benefit from a few hours of extra daylight provided by plant grow-lights.

There are mist systems, self-irrigation units, automatic blinds and lighting operated by a staggering array of technological inventions, such as photo-electric cells, moisture sensitive fibres, solar panels and so on. The deeper you get into the intricacies of greenhouse gardening, the more you will want to find out about these things, but I haven't reached that point myself – yet.

LEFT: Paint and netting are alternative methods to shade a greenhouse.

GREENHOUSE GARDENING BASICS

NO MATTER WHAT YOU EVENTUALLY END UP using the greenhouse for, be it growing African violets or crops of winter lettuce, you will benefit from knowing how to propagate plants.

Propagation

There are few things more pleasurable than watching a tiny seed or stubby cutting mature into a stunning plant except, perhaps, the knowledge that the beautiful plant you've grown hardly cost you a penny. Propagation is one of the most rewarding of garden enterprises and a greenhouse makes it that much easier to raise new plants for the garden and for your greenhouse collections.

Success with propagating depends on keeping the seedlings or cuttings moist, warm and provided with adequate light while they grow. The greenhouse will help you to ensure there is plenty of light, but the moisture and warmth must come from a propagating unit, because it would be wasteful and prohibitively expensive to try and heat an entire greenhouse to the correct degree of warmth.

ABOVE: The first horticultural aid a gardener should invest in is an electric propagating unit with a soil-warming cable.

RIGHT: Propagation will help you to achieve extravagant displays, such as the marvellous array of hanging baskets and containers shown here.

The simplest form of propagating unit is the plastic bag fitted over the cuttings or pot-sown seeds. This can be made more sophisticated by making a coathanger-wire frame to hold the bag upright and keep it from touching the leaves of the cuttings, and securing the bag around the rim of the pot with a rubberband or piece of string. Alternatively, you can stick to the basics and simply put the pot in the bag, tucking the opening under the pot to keep it closed. Use a large enough bag to leave plenty of head space above the cuttings and every so often give it a flick to knock condensation off the sides of the bag. This is the method I use and it never fails.

The other simple propagator, which I use most frequently for soft cuttings, is the 2-litre plastic drink bottle cut in half to form two clear plastic domes, which fit neatly into the rims of 7.5 cm/3 in flowerpots.

Moving up the scale of sophistication – but not too far – is the seed tray with a moulded, clear plastic cover. The covers can be bought separately to fit the various sizes of seed trays or they can be purchased as complete propagating units. There are variations on this theme, such as cell trays and covers enabling you to sow each seed or root each cutting in isolation from its neighbours; the advantage here is that they lessen root disturbance when transplanting. Seed trays can also be covered with cling film, but you must take care to remove this the minute seedlings poke their heads above the soil.

These systems are fine to use when you do not have access to a heated propagating unit, so are satisfactory to use during the warm summer months and into late summer when many soft cuttings are taken. But if you plan to sow seed in early spring or are trying to root plants that demand bottom heat you will have to move up to the more advanced technologies of soil-warming cables and self-contained propagating units that have built-in heating units in their bases.

Units such as this usually have a deep plastic tray with a warming cable embedded in the bottom. The base is covered with a layer of moist silver sand to help distribute the heat evenly across the surface on which the pots or trays are placed. The plastic cover is put in place, the thermostatic control is set and, before you know it, roots strike out and seedlings leap into action. It can be difficult to get the heat accurately adjusted – as I know, having steam-cooked a trayful or two of vegetable seeds in my early days.

The best system, however, is the purpose-made propagating bench. This is a section of staging with sides raised at least 23 cm/9 in around all four edges. The bottom of this box is covered with a 5 cm/2 in layer of silver sand over which the soil-warming cable is laid. A thermostat is put in place and another layer of silver sand is spread over the cable and thermostat sensor. The cover of the unit is made from a sheet of clear polythene stretched over a frame made to the same dimensions as the base.

Cuttings do best if they are kept moist, and the best way to ensure this is to fit a misting spray unit into the bench. The spray head creates a moist vapour around the cuttings and it only sprays when the controlling device indicates that the ambient moisture level around the plants has dropped. There are various kits available, so follow the manufacturer's instructions when installing the unit.

ABOVE: There are automatic watering systems, but beginners will no doubt want to rely on the good old-fashioned watering can fitted with a fine rose so seedlings are not washed away. Hand-watering does keep the gardener in touch with the condition of the plants much better than an automatic system, which is perhaps better suited to professional growers.

SEED-SOWING

This is the fundamental method of raising new plants and is used mostly to raise vegetables and annual and biennial flowers for the garden. However, most species of plant can be raised from seeds. Bear in mind, though, that if the plant you are wanting to increase is a hybrid cultivar, seed saved from it will not come true and look like its parent. Instead, it will look

BELOW: A greenhouse reaches its full potential when used for propagating as well as growing exotic plants.

ABOVE: **When sowing many types of plants in the greenhouse it is advisable to have labels on hand to keep track of what you are growing.**

BELOW: **As the seedlings grow they must be pricked out into individual pots and spaced along the staging to give them plenty of room to develop into sturdy plants.**

like one or the other of its parents or at least have different colouring. In fact, even seed saved from species which will come true may have variations of colour intensity, flower size and so on. This is quite interesting to watch for, as you may be able to develop your own especially good form of a favourite plant.

The best way to sow seed is to fill a pot or tray with moist seed compost, firm it gently into the container and then water well. Add fungicide to the water first to help prevent damping off (rotting) of emerging seedlings. Scatter the seed thinly and evenly over the surface of the soil then sieve a fine layer of compost over the seed. Water gently (with more dilute fungicide) and put the pot into a plastic bag or cover the tray. The seed should germinate in seven to ten days. As soon as you see the seed is beginning to germinate, and is pushing through the soil, move the pot into the light.

When the seedlings are large enough to handle, which will be when the first true leaves (as opposed to the seed leaves) develop, lift them gently from the compost using the end of a pencil or other small tool. Always hold a seedling by one of the leaves, never by the stem. If the leaf breaks it will be replaced by another, but if the stem is damaged it means the plant is lost.

Prick out the individual seedlings of large plants such as melons, cucumbers, peppers, aubergines and tomatoes into separate pots. Lettuces, herbs, marigolds, other small annuals and so on can be pricked out into rows in trays. Don't crowd them though; they need room to develop into strong plants and if planted less than 2.5 cm/1 in apart they will become weak and straggly as they fight each other for food and light. In a standard seed tray, about five plants across and six down (30 plants) is a good average.

After transplanting, keep the seedlings in the greenhouse for a few days and then, as the weather warms, begin to move them outside for a few hours each day, increasing the time they spend in the fresh air as the days increase in warmth. This is called hardening off and is an essential part of the process of raising plants from seed. It is not a good idea to transfer a young plant from the sheltered cloister of the greenhouse straight into the knock-about world of the garden. The shock might well be too much for its underdeveloped system.

CUTTINGS

Soft cuttings are made from the new season's growth taken during spring through summer. Select healthy, new, non-flowering shoots and collect the cuttings in the early morning while they are still fresh, before the sun and breeze have had their drying effect. As you collect the cuttings, put them into a plastic bag into which you have sprinkled a few drops of water as it is essential to keep the cuttings moist.

On the potting bench, prepare the compost-filled pots and trays as for seed-sowing, but add extra grit or horticultural vermiculite to the mix to make sure it has quite an open texture; do this even if the compost you purchase says it is for cuttings. I usually add extra grit in a ratio of one potful of grit to two of compost. Juvenile roots will find it easier to develop in an open compost; compaction of damp compost would cause the cutting to rot.

Next, look at the cutting. The point where the leaves attach to the stem is called the leaf node; you must trim away the stem below this point as cleanly as you can without squashing the end. Use a sharp knife rather than scissors. You should then trim away all but the uppermost two pairs of leaves; the reason for this is that you want to prevent the cutting losing moisture and moisture is lost through the leaves. However, the cutting must retain a life support system of a few leaves to continue the process of photosynthesis. When trimming the leaves off, take care not to damage the stem.

Dip the cut end into hormone rooting powder or solution. You don't have to use this treatment, but it helps. Shake off any excess rooting agent; too much would kill the cutting.

Use a sharpened stick (or pencil) to dibble a hole into the potting compost and then insert the cutting to about one-third of its depth. Firm the compost around the cutting and water in with a fungicide solution. Put the pots and trays into the covered propagator (without bottom heat if it is quite warm out) and shade from bright sunlight.

It will take about four to five weeks for the cuttings to root; you can test if they have rooted by tugging gently at the top growth, and if it fights back, remaining firmly in its pot, you will know it has roots. The pots and trays can then be moved out of the propagator to harden off the cuttings before potting on into individual pots.

ABOVE: **When propagating from cuttings, you will need to have hormone-rooting powder or solution, a sharp knife for trimming, clean pots and a loose compost prepared specially for cuttings.**

Semi-ripe cuttings are taken later in the summer when the new season's growth has begun to harden off and go woody near the base. Semi-ripe cuttings should be about the size of a pencil and are removed from the parent plant by tugging sharply downward so that they come away with a small tongue of old wood at the base. This tapering little flap is called the heel, and should be trimmed neatly across the end to leave only a tiny bit of old wood at the base of the cutting. It will form into a callus from which the roots will develop.

Trim away all the leaves except the uppermost three or four and continue as for soft cuttings. Semi-ripe cuttings, also called half-ripe or heel cuttings, will root in much cooler conditions so can be left to root on the greenhouse staging.

RIGHT: Once the cuttings have established root systems, they can be potted on individually and removed from the protective cover of the propagating unit and stood in the open, but still in the greenhouse, to harden off; keep them shaded on sunny days.

Internodal cuttings are taken in summer and the shoot is trimmed to leave 2.5 cm/1 in of stem above and below a leaf node selected for the healthy, fat bud it holds at the junction of the leaf and main stem. Treat as for a soft cutting, but leave at least one leaf and the bud, then pot up the cutting, burying the node below the surface of the compost. Roots will develop at the base of the node.

Leaf blade cuttings are made from healthy young leaves removed from the parent plant during midsummer. Turn the leaf upside down on a clean surface and, with a sharp knife, make small incisions across the main veins, cutting through to the other side. Turn the leaf right-side up and lay it on a tray full of moist potting compost making sure that the cut veins are in contact with the surface of the soil. Use a few clean pebbles to hold the leaf in place, cover the tray with a sheet of glass or cling film and put in a warm, shady place or else in a propagating unit with gentle bottom heat. In a few weeks, roots will form at the wound sites and new plantlets will begin to emerge on the uppermost side of the leaf. Pot them up when they are big enough to handle. This is the method most often used to propagate ornamental-leaf begonias and streptocarpus.

The other method of leaf blade cutting is to cut the leaf into 'squares taking care that a vein runs through the centre of each square. Begonia sections can be laid flat on the compost and streptocarpus can be inserted upright to half their depth in the compost; this method can also be used to propagate mother-in-law's tongue and Christmas and Easter cactus, except with the cacti there is no need to cut the leaves into pieces; simply detach a segment and insert it to half its depth in compost. It will root before you know it.

Leaf petiole cuttings are generally used to propagate African violets. Remove a healthy leaf and cut the stem of the leaf (this is the petiole) to about 2.5 cm/1 in long. Dip the cut end in rooting powder and insert in the compost taking care that the leaf does not touch the soil. Put the stem

BELOW: African violets are a favourite plant among collectors; this is 'Olga'. They are easy to increase from leaf petiole cuttings.

RIGHT: The spider plant is a common house plant that is easy to propogate from the little plantlets at the end of the long runners sent out by the parent plant.

BELOW: In the early spring a vegetable gardener gets a head start sowing tomato seeds, beans and chitting potato seed in trays.

in so that it is held at a shallow angle, not upright. Water with a fungicide solution and put into the propagator, shaded from direct sunlight.

RUNNERS

These are new growths sent out by the parent plant and appear at the end of long stems. Many of the saxifrages, the ubiquitous spider plant and strawberries are the most familiar runner-producing plants. This method of propagation couldn't be easier; just peg the end of the runner down into a pot of compost. The baby plant will root happily and the umbilical runner can then be severed. If you have many runners and wish to root them all, it might not be easy to attach each one to a pot of compost. Instead, separate the babies from the parent plant, dibble them into a tray of compost, water with fungicide and put into a warm, covered propagator where they will take root in a few weeks.

DIVISION

This is another method of increasing stock from a parent plant by uprooting it and cutting it into sections. As many herbaceous perennials age, they die out in the centre but continue to make new growth around the perimeter of the clump. It is from here that new plants are taken; cut them into reasonable-sized pieces, making sure that each one has at least two or three growth points. Grasp the roots in a bunch as though you were gathering a handful of hair for a ponytail and trim away any ends that protrude. Dahlias, irises and other tubers and rhizomes can be treated in this fashion; simply cutting off pieces or sectioning them, dusting the cut edges with fungicide and then potting up to take root. Some pot plants will develop into clusters of many plantlets, which can simply be pulled apart and potted up individually. Dividing one old plant into a dozen new ones is especially satisfying.

Offsets are the reproductive structures found in some bulbs and corms. Unearth a mature bulb and you will see several smaller bulbs crowding around the base. Pick them off and set them into trays or pots to grow on.

Scales removed from lily bulbs and inserted upright into trays of moist compost will eventually produce small bulbs at their base. Some lilies also produce tiny bulbils along the flower stem in the leaf axils (the place between the leaf petiole and the main stem).

Bulbs produced from these methods will take several years to come to flower, during which time they must be fed and watered regularly.

AIR LAYERING

This is the way to create new plants from tall, leggy subjects such as rubber plants and shrubby gems such as rhododendron and azalea species and cultivars. It is a method that relies on the plant's natural inclination to make roots wherever a branch touches the ground, and is best done during late summer.

Select a healthy looking, long, straight side shoot that is beginning to mature. Using a sharp knife, make a wound in the centre of the stem by slicing along the stem towards the growing tip, lifting the narrow tongue of bark. Use a clean splinter of wood (a split matchstick is handy) to hold the flap up while you dust the wound with rooting compound.

To create a moist atmosphere around the wound, wrap it snugly in damp (not dripping) sphagnum moss, which you can obtain from a garden centre. Then wrap this in plastic to prevent it drying out, sealing both ends with lengths of twist-tie. Keep the parent plant warm and watered. Be very patient, and in several months you should see roots emerging through the moss. You can then sever the shoot from the parent plant, making the cut cleanly just below the root mass, and pot it up to grow on.

ABOVE: **Bubble plastic insulation against the greenhouse glazing assists the gardener in growing a wide range of tender plants.**

With every one of these methods, it is essential to use fungicide when watering in initially and to always make sure the knives and tools you use are scrupulously clean; likewise the pots and trays you use. I always wash pots (clay and plastic) and scrub trays in a mild solution of household disinfectant and dip the scalpel used for trimming and preparing cuttings in surgical spirit.

Pots and Potting

Now is probably the time to say a few words about pots and potting. Traditionally, clay or terracotta pots were the gardeners' favourites for growing greenhouse plants. They are certainly mine, as the colour and texture go so well with the flowers and leaves of the various plants I grow. But clay is porous so it dries out easily in the moist, warm atmosphere of a greenhouse. Clay pots also get covered in green algae and must be scrubbed clean from time to time.

Plastic pots help the compost to retain moisture better, they remain clean and after time and use the shiny finish becomes dull and scratched,

BELOW: You will need a selection of seed trays and pots when potting; some trays are designed to provide individual plugs so that the plant roots are not disturbed too often by pricking out and potting on.

so it is not so glaringly plastic. They are lighter in weight than clay pots, so may have the tendency to tip over if plants become top heavy, but if you pot on properly this should not be a problem. Unlike clay pots, which have only one drainage hole, plastic pots have a number of small holes around the base and so it is not necessary, as it is with clay pots, to use a layer of broken crocks in the bottom of the pot to assist drainage.

Pots come in sizes ranging from 5 cm/2 in to 45 cm/18 in in diameter. Round pots are best for mature plants, but I recommend using small square pots for raising cuttings and seedlings because you will be able to fit more pots neatly into a tray. For mass production you might consider using poly-bags, which are like miniature dustbin bags but with drainage

BELOW: Try to avoid overcrowding in the greenhouse as this can greatly enhance the risk of disease.

ABOVE: The cherry tomato 'Sungold' is renowned for the sweetness of its fruit, as well as for being a heavy cropper. It does very well in pots in the greenhouse.

holes. These are economical, but rather difficult to get used to using since you have to be sure to fill the flimsy bag evenly to avoid air pockets around the plant's roots.

For seed-sowing you can buy peat blocks that are compressed and dried; soak them in water and they swell to form a small receptacle for an individual seed. Once the plant has grown enough to be put out in the garden, or into a pot, the whole thing can just be popped into the compost, avoiding any disturbance to the roots.

POTTING UP

When a plant is ready to be transferred from its nursery quarters to a larger pot or tray, where it will spend at least the next year of its life, you must pot it up carefully, using a suitable compost; perhaps adding a slow-release granular fertiliser. Be firm but gentle when anchoring the root ball into the new home so as not to damage the roots.

You will be aware of whether or not the plant likes acid soil or alkaline; free-draining, sandy loam or moisture-retentive, humus-rich soil. So select the potting compost accordingly; you can get purpose-blended composts for African violets, rhododendrons and cacti, as well as general-purpose houseplant composts. Osmacote is a typical and useful general-purpose fertiliser with a soluble coating that gradually disintegrates, releasing the nutrients. There are also foliar feeds that you should use regularly when watering the plant, spraying the leaves which then absorb the nutrients.

Use clean, undamaged pots and, if it is a collection, try to use all the same sort of pot to give a sense of unity to the array of plants you are displaying. Some plants may be climbers, in which case you will need to use a support; there are all sorts available, from a simple thin cane to an elaborate wirework trellis. There are a number of different ways of attaching the plant to the support if it is not a self-supporter; wire twists can be used, but you must check that the stem is not growing so thick that the wire is cutting into it. Natural and plastic raffia, soft string and simple wire rings are also useful. Always put the support in place before you fill in around the rootball with the potting compost; that way you can see that you are not damaging the roots, and will know that the support is deep enough into the pot to be secure.

If you are using clay pots, put a layer of broken crocks (pieces of an old flowerpot) in the base to aid drainage over the single hole; plastic pots don't need this. Put a layer of compost over the crocks or in the bottom of the pot. Water the cuttings or seedlings and then lift the young plant from its tray using an old fork or a special dibber tool, remembering to hold it by the leaf, not the stem. Position it centrally in the pot and then fill with compost around the root ball. Fill to half-full with soil, then tap the pot firmly around the sides to settle the soil and finish filling the pot. Water in using a fungicide solution.

POTTING ON

Eventually, the plant will have to be potted on when its root ball becomes too large for the size of container it is in. The plant may be potbound by this point, with the roots growing out through the drainage hole. Some flowering plants, such as ornamental pelargoniums and African violets, perform best when they are slightly potbound, so don't be in too much of a hurry to pot on.

When the time has come, though, select a pot that is the next size up, not one that is two or three times larger. Invert the potted plant and tap the rim gently on the edge of the potting bench to knock the plant out of its old pot. You may want to tease some of the old compost away from the roots, loosening the surface of the root ball so that the new compost can be worked in among the roots. Place the plant in the new pot and fill with fresh compost, firming gently with your fingertips as you work. Fill to within 2.5 cm/1 in of the rim, give the pot a sharp tap around the sides to settle the compost and add more compost to bring the level up to about 1cm/1/2 in of the pot rim. Water in using a fine rose on the watering can.

ABOVE: **All gardeners love watching a plant develop from a grain of seed to a mature flowering beauty; it is also a joy to save as much money as you are able to when you grow your own bedding, such as these primulas.**

In time, the plant will reach its mature size or the size to which you wish to keep it by pruning the top growth and roots. It can stay in the same pot, but will have to be repotted each year to replenish the compost. This is best done in the spring before the plant comes into active growth. Knock it from its pot and scrap off as much of the old compost as you can. This will loosen the roots, which can be pruned with a clean knife or secateurs. If the plant is large, it's a good idea to scrape away at least 5 cm/2 in of old top soil, so that you can replace the top layer with new compost. This method is called top-dressing and can be done if repotting is not entirely necessary. Next, check the crocks, put a layer of fresh compost in the bottom of the pot (if you're reusing the old pot, wash it first), put the plant in place and then fill and firm new compost around the root ball. Water in well. In fact, you can stand the plant in a basin of water to let it soak for several hours to make sure the root ball and new compost are thoroughly moist.

Pests and Diseases

All the ills that attack plants in the garden will also play havoc with plants in a greenhouse, so you must be even more militant in your efforts to keep your greenhouse garden healthy. The best way to do this is prevention – keep the greenhouse clean. Each year, on a sunny day in early spring, clear all the plants out of the house, remove the staging too if you can and wash

RIGHT: **Tuberous-root begonias are highly ornamental and can be brought on in the greenhouse to provide a stunning dash of colour in container displays outdoors.**

LEFT: Good hygiene is essential in keeping the greenhouse free of pests and disease. After one crop is finished, the house must be cleaned out thoroughly before another crop is installed. This is particularly true of tomatoes, especially if they become infested with whitefly, which they so often do when under glass.

it down with a general-purpose disinfectant garden cleanser such as Armillatox. Wash the algae buildup from the glass and frames, clear plant debris from the floor and corners, where it gathers like dust balls under a bed, sweep the floor and generally spruce up the area.

On the staging, remove capillary matting, gravel and so on if it has become grotty and replace with new material or else wash and rinse it thoroughly (dump gravel into a large tub or basin and fill with water, debris will float to the top and can be drained off).

Check the pots and tidy them up too if necessary; check over the plants themselves and pot on or repot as necessary.

Throughout the year keep a close eye on the plants; any which become diseased should be removed and dealt with in quarantine. But the best plan is to follow good horticultural practices; keep the plants healthy by feeding regularly and watering wisely (not too much). An ounce of prevention is worth a pound of cure in the greenhouse.

ROOT AND STEM DAMAGE

Ants are common garden pests that churn up the soil in containers, disturbing the root systems.

Cutworms are dirty, sludge-green pests found just below the soil surface. They gnaw through the stems at the base of plants, severing plants from their roots.

BELOW: Greenfly aphids attacking a tulip.

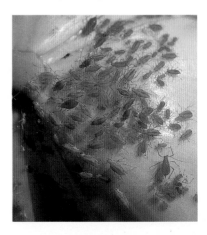

ABOVE: **The vine weevil will attack the corms, tubers and bulbs of ornamental plants.**

Eelworms are pin-thin worms that feed on the inside of stems and roots of plants.

Leatherjackets are khaki-grey grubs found in the soil; they are the larval stage of the daddy long-legs and feed on plant roots.

Mice and rats are the familiar rodents which feast on bulbs (especially crocus) and seedlings.

Root aphids are the sap-sucking aphids found on the roots of infected plants.

Slugs and snails are the familiar garden pests which live in damp, shady places and, in the case of slugs, just below the soil. They eat all plant parts.

RIGHT: **Slugs leave a slimy trail and gnaw holes in leaves and through stems.**

Vine weevils are off-white grubs that eat corms, tubers and bulbs.

LEAF AND STEM DAMAGE

Aphids (include blackfly and greenfly) are small flying insects that suck sap from stems. Most often found in thick clusters on the tips of succulent new growth.

Caterpillars are the familiar garden pests that transform into moths and butterflies, but before doing so feast on the leaves and stems of many sorts of plants.

Earwigs are glossy, brown segmented insects with rear-end pincers that chew up leaves, flower buds and petals.

Flea beetles are the tiny black bugs that jump from foliage, emitting a clicking sound as they do so. They are particularly partial to members of the brassica family.

Leaf miners are recognised by the silvery track-lines they leave trailed across leaves and also from lumps and bumps on the leaf surface.

Mealy bugs are small, white insects that create a protective covering of white 'wool' around themselves as they feed.

Red spider mites are barely visible to the naked eye; attack can be identified by leaves yellowing and turning brown and the presence of fine, white webbing between leaf and stem.

Scale insects have attacked when pinhead-sized, brown bumps appear on the undersides of leaves.

Thrips are small yellow, brown or black insects, which cause spotting and mottling of leaves.

Whiteflies are minute, white flying insects, which are a real greenhouse problem, causing leaves to yellow and wilt and depositing a black residue on ripening tomatoes and the stems and foliage of greenhouse-grown plants.

Woodlice are little, armadillo-type insects with segmented shells and many legs, which cause damage to developing seed leaves.

These pests can be treated by combined chemical sprays, which will deal with a combination of pests; or with specialised treatments, such as fumigating cones to take care of whitefly. Many insecticides are

ABOVE: Aphids will quickly disfigure a wide range of flowers and vegetables.

BELOW: Whiteflies are particularly difficult to dislodge once they become established.

available in powder form and these are especially useful against ants and woodlice. Often these insecticides are systemic, meaning they enter the circulatory system of the plant so that as the bug chews the plant or sucks the sap, it also ingests the poison. When using insecticides, be sure to follow the the manufacturer's instructions.

DISEASES

Botrytis (grey mould), mildew, root rot, sooty mould, stem rot, wilt, leaf spot and black spot are mostly fungal diseases and there are a wide range of sprays available to treat them.

WARNING: It is extremely important to use insecticides and fungicides with caution, following the manufacturer's instructions to the letter. Some of them are highly irritant and will be indicated as being so by a large black cross on the label. If you get any on your skin, wash it off immediately. Protect your eyes by wearing goggles or shields and cover your nose and mouth with a mask or folded kerchief. Never use chemicals when children and pets are about and always store them safely – do not mix solutions and store for future use in soda bottles or jam jars. As always, keep all chemicals out of the reach of children.

BIOLOGICAL CONTROLS

Many gardeners prefer to work with nature when cultivating their plants, using natural methods such as companion planting (planting together those plants which are purported to be mutually beneficial), making natural insecticides from certain plants (for example making a spray from onions and chilli peppers steeped in water to combat red spider mite), and introducing biological controls to keep the garden and greenhouse pest-free.

ABOVE: Mildew, also known as botrytis, ruins foliage and fruit and will wither flower buds on the stem, as shown on the strawberries and rose buds pictured above.

Biological control has been gaining ground over the past few years and is similar in principal to setting a thief to catch a thief, by releasing beneficial insects as pest-predators to control infestations. This method is particularly well-suited to the greenhouse because the closed environment is warm and moist, providing ideal living conditions for the unwanted predators, most of which are so small you will hardly be able to see them in action.

However, there are a few house-warming rules to follow before you welcome these beneficial visitors. Biological controls are mostly available through mail order suppliers and orders should be made in the spring, when the weather begins to warm up, as some are temperature sensitive. They will arrive with a manual so read the instructions carefully; some biological controls can be expensive and you won't want to reinvest because you've mistreated the first arrivals. Clearly, you will not want to risk poisoning the beneficial insects as well as pests, so don't spray with insecticides for at least a month before they are introduced.

If you run into problems with this, use an organic, soft soap insecticide, but try to hold off in the weeks prior to delivery of the control insects. After introduction, they may take up to four weeks to establish effective working colonies; light shade, high levels of humidity and placing plants close together on benches and staging will all encourage the control insects to spread easily and quickly among the plants.

TYPES OF BIOLOGICAL CONTROL

Bacillus thuringiensis is actually a bacteria that is used as a powder dissolved into a spray solution. The spores form crystals that poison the gut of insect pests, but are not in the least toxic to humans or animals. It is especially good for caterpillar pests.

Cryptolaemus montrouzeri is the Australian ladybird and is an effective control for mealy bugs, but does require plenty of sunshine and high temperatures to live – at least 20°C/68°F.

Encarsia formosa is a microscopic, but mighty powerful wasp that targets whitefly. It is supplied in the pupal stage, attached to a card and should be

BELOW: Biological controls include predators such as the Australian ladybird, which feeds on mealy bugs.

ABOVE: Phytoseiulus - all biological controls must be used exactly according to the instructions.

BELOW: Australian ladybird

introduced the moment whitefly are discovered. Place the card among the worst infested plants, so the encarsia have a ready food supply in their early stages; they only feed on juvenile whitefly, so you will probably need to do three introductions about two weeks apart in early spring. To deal with adult whitefly (should any escape) you can use yellow sticky cards hung above the infested plants to trap the insects in flight. (Thrips can be controlled using blue sticky cards.)

Nematodes are used against soil-borne pests and there are various sorts available to treat vine weevils and slugs, but not snails, by watering them into the soil during spring or autumn so they can attack the grubs and juveniles of these pests.

Phytoseiulus persimilis is used against red spider mites, and since it requires cool temperatures is used during spring and autumn. It is usually provided on a withered leaf that is then hung among the infested plants.

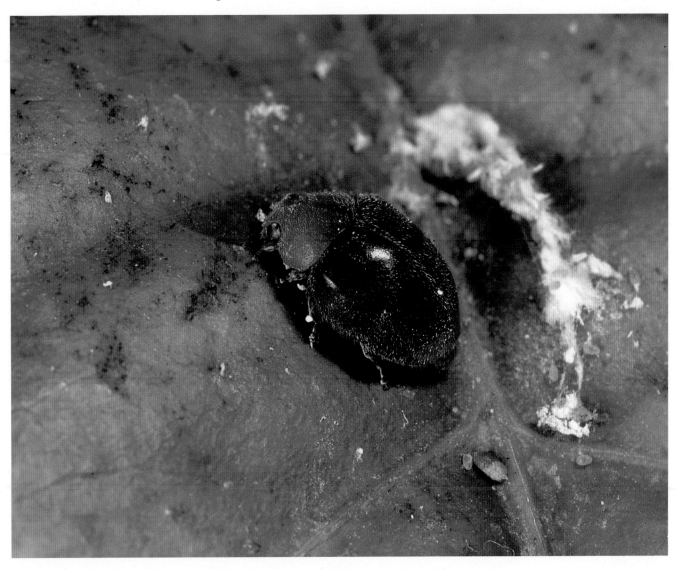

GREENHOUSE PLANTS

THE ROUTINE OF MY OWN GREENHOUSE will probably give you the best indication of a general programme since I use the house year round for growing just about anything I can get my hands on. I use my greenhouse to grow special vegetable crops, propagate tender exotics and many hardy herbaceous species (especially hostas and grasses) for the garden, and to overwinter collections of succulents, citrus, scented-leaf geraniums and assorted non-hardy treasures that I lift from the garden.

I live in a region that has plenty of sunshine, low levels of rainfall and a fairly moderate annual climate, but the growing season is short. My family like sweetcorn, sweet peppers, beefsteak tomatoes, basil, and charantais melons. So to raise these crops in my short-season garden, I start everything in the greenhouse, sowing the seed during early spring, pricking out by late spring and setting the corn (an early ripening variety) out in the garden after I'm sure the last frost is past. Everything else is raised in the greenhouse in grow bags.

Many half-hardy exotics that I grow in the garden during the summer and early autumn are propagated (along with anything else I care to increase) with soft cuttings and semi-ripe cuttings during mid to late summer. Perennial seed is collected and sown if appropriate, or else reserved until the spring.

By the time autumn arrives, the vegetable crops are eaten or harvested and stored, freeing the greenhouse space for the emigration of the tender plants from the garden and potted up cuttings and so on.

During winter, the fan heater keeps the frost out and I check daily to see that things are in order; clearing away fallen leaves and generally trying to keep the greenhouse and plants tidy and healthy. When early spring arrives, I have the annual cleaning of glass and staging so that the cycle begins again in fresh surroundings.

RIGHT: The exotic flowering plant datura, angel's trumpets, which is poisonous if eaten.

BELOW: Use a greenhouse to provide sunny-climate food, such as tomotoes.

Vegetables

Although you can grow any vegetable in a greenhouse – and that is what many organic growers do to ensure complete non-contamination of the soil and to assist biological control of pests and diseases – for the amateur gardener it only makes sense to grow choice crops as mentioned earlier. By choice crops I mean things that are difficult to grow outdoors in your

LEFT: Cantaloupe melons are climbers so will need support.

climate, or perhaps something to savour out of season, such as early straw-berries or melons.

Grow bags are handy, self-contained units full of compost enriched with a careful balance of nutrients for vegetable crops. The instructions for their use are printed on the outside of most bags, but generally it amounts to setting the plants into the prepared opening in the bag, pro-viding it with support, and then watering it regularly and feeding as nec-essary. At the end of each season, you can add the compost to the heap to recycle it or scatter it on the garden and dig it lightly into the soil.

Alternatively, you can prepare a permanent bed along one edge of the greenhouse, digging the soil to a minimum of 45 cm/18 in deep and incorporating plenty of humus or well-rotted garden compost to improve the soil condition. It also helps to dig in at least 5 cm/2 in of gravel into the bottom of the trench to improve drainage. Crops can then be grown directly into this prepared bed, but if you intend to grow the same crop, such as tomatoes, year after year, you will have to replace the soil regularly to ensure that it does not become depleted of vital nutrients and trace elements.

BELOW: Tomatoes crop better if they have the extra root space that ring culture provides.

Seed-Sown Ornamentals: Annuals and Bedding Plants

Most of these plants are sown in the spring to be planted out during the early summer. Some varieties, however, can be sown in late summer or autumn to provide flowering plants indoors during winter or early spring. To do this you must provide the young plants with adequate heat and light to sustain steady, even growth and good ventilation to avoid disease.

Half-Hardy and Tender Perennials

Being able to cultivate these flowering ornamentals is one of the joys of owning a greenhouse; nothing quite equals the perfume of an orange tree in flower or the sight of a magnificent angel's trumpet (*Datura sauveolens*) in full flower. **WARNING:** Datura is poisonous if the leaves, seeds or flowers are eaten.

Most half-hardy and tender perennials will survive a minimum winter temperature of 10°C/50°F, but there are others, especially tropical and subtropical plants, such as bromeliads, orchids and so on that require greater warmth. So when establishing your collection, bear this in mind and determine just how warm you are prepared to keep the greenhouse. However, even though a plant will accept a minimum temperature, it really shouldn't be kept in the cold for too long or the flower quality will deteriorate, as will the plant. (A useful tip to remember: if a tender plant

ABOVE: **Tomato 'Alicante' is a reliable cropper for grow bag culture.**

RIGHT: **Cyclamen are favourite ornamental plants easily raised from seed in the greenhouse.**

becomes frosted overnight, spraying it with cold water before the sun touches it may help it to recover.)

Generally, plant health benefits from keeping the leaves as well as the greenhouse glass clean so the process of photosynthesis is not impeded. Wipe both the plant's leaves and the glass over occasionally with a soft, damp cloth. There are proprietary sprays available to cleanse and impart a shine, but a buildup of spray residue would not be a good thing for the plants. During warm spring showers move the plants outdoors as they will benefit from the rain and the fresh air.

Not all plants enjoy full, bright sunshine all day long, so do ascertain whether the plants in your collection like indirect light – where they receive only ambient light – or no direct sunlight or partial sun, which means they are shaded during midday when the sun is at its highest. Full sun explains itself, but there are a few plants (cacti and succulents among them) that enjoy a baking under glass.

Finally, you should collect rainwater to water greenhouse plants as they will benefit from pure water as opposed to the chemical concoction that comes out of most taps.

Suggested Plants to Grow

The list of plants you wish to grow in your greenhouse could be infinite, so this selection concentrates on only one area – half-hardy and tender ornamentals – and are ones which I have enjoyed growing or have admired in friends' greenhouses. It includes some bulbs and annuals, but mostly it is shrubs and herbaceous, perennial-type plants. These plants are dual purpose, as most of them can be put out in the garden during the summer and brought into the house for short spells during win-ter, thus spreading the enjoyment you have from them across the seasons. Do regard this selection as a sampler, something to inspire you when filling your greenhouse. Unless otherwise stated the minimum winter temperatures are 10°C/50°F.

ABOVE: *Begonia elatior* is a tuberous-rooted begonia.

RIGHT: *Begonia elatior*, known for their spectacular leaves, add a special touch to greenhouses.

African violets see **Saintpaulia**

Asparagus densiflorus (syn. *A. sprengeri*)
Trailing perennial with spiky, glossy green leaves covering the stems, giving the plant a fluffy appearance. Requires moist soil in partial shade to do well.

Begonia rex
There are many sorts of begonias; some are grown for their lovely, showy flowers and are widely used in container plantings, but this particular group is known for its leaves, which are spectacular. There is a huge range of shape, colours and markings. Partial shade and moist soil is required.

Bougainvillea
A woody-stemmed, climbing plant that is covered in carnival-coloured flowers, which look like they are cut from tissue paper. 'Amethyst',

'Flamingo Pink', 'Golden Glow', 'Royal Purple' and 'Scarlet Queen' are just a few of the many cultivars available. They need full sun and well-drained soil; keep completely dry during the dormant season.

Bromeliads

These include a number of lovely plants all belonging to the family Bromeliaceae, including tillandsias, guzmanias, billbergias and aechmeas. Generally they all look like a cross between pineapple tops and agaves. Most form rosettes of leaves that are long and taper to a sharp point. The leaves can be either broad or very narrow, grey-green to dark green, while some are variegated white, cream or shades of pink. They should be grown in quite small pots in full sun and well-drained soil; be careful to water only sparingly.

Cacti

These familiar plants are fun to collect because of their widely varied shapes and forms; they are also a pleasure when they flower. Give partial shade in summer and full sun in winter; keep the gritty compost on the dry side.

Cineraria

A showy flowering plant, which is good for winter displays. Usually treated as an annual, it is easily grown from seed sown during late spring to midsummer. Requires partial shade and moist soil.

ABOVE: A cacti collection on staging, including specimens of the barrel cactus.

RIGHT: *Echinocactus grusonii* **(top) and** *Gymnocalycium mihanowichii* **(bottom).**

BELOW: Cineraria is an annual bedding plant that can be raised from seed in the greenhouse.

Citrus (orange, lemon, grapefruit)
Evergreen trees that produce the most deliciously scented flowers as well as juicy fruit. Grow in full sun in gritty soil. Do not overwater during winter and feed with a high-potash fertiliser in early spring.

Clivia
A rhizomatous perennial with broad leaves and tumbels of red flowers. Flowers best if potbound and should be dead-headed to conserve strength for the next season's flowering. Requires partial shade; water well during the growing season, but keep quite dry during the winter.

Coleus blumei (now known as **Solenostemon** or **Plectranthus**)
Produces a wide range of striking foliage forms. The plant forms a bushy shape and is quite fast-growing – a leaf or cutting placed in a glass of water will soon form roots. Partial shade in moist soil is required.

ABOVE: Citrus of all kinds, including kumquats, tangerines and limes, as well as the familiar oranges and lemons (above) can be grown and cropped in the greenhouse.

LEFT: Colourful coleus is used in bedding displays in the garden and also as a house plant – their foliage is striking.

RIGHT: x *citrofortunella mitis*.

Cyclamen persicum

A tuberous-rooted perennial usually grown from seed sown in the late summer for winter and spring flowering. The root can be retained after flowering and, if kept in a dry, shady place, should flower again the next season. Requires partial shade and moist soil during flowering.

Datura x candida

Commonly known as angel's trumpets this is a semi-evergreen shrub that can reach 3 m/9 ft, but only in the most favourable conditions. Generally, in a greenhouse specimen it will reach only 1.5 m/5 ft. The

ABOVE: *Cyclamen persicum*, the Persian cyclamen

LEFT: *Datura* x *candida* syn. *Brugmansia* x. *candida,* angel's trumpets, is sweetly scented but poisonous if eaten.

ABOVE: *Datura versicolor –* **beautiful but poisonous if any part of the plant is eaten.**

BELOW: **Fuchsia 'Lisa'.**

pendulous, trumpet-shaped flowers are strongly scented in the evening, so it is a good plant to move out onto a terrace during the summer. It likes full sun and well-drained soil, a little on the dry side. As mentioned before, datura is poisonous if leaves, seeds or flowers are eaten.

Epiphyllum oxypetallum

This is the renowned night-blooming cactus; the flowers develop slowly and, on the night they bloom, the huge white flowers give off a deep, pervasive perfume. During Edwardian times it was a tradition to entertain on the evening the cactus was expected to flower in order to share the event with your guests. It likes partial shade and rich, moist soil.

Felicia amelloïdes

This tender plant with its sky-blue daisy flowers is often grown for windowbox displays, but can be an unusual colour addition to the flower border. Raise from cuttings taken in the early summer for winter flowers in the greenhouse, or in late summer for spring displays. Requires full sun in well-drained soil.

Fuchsia

There are many flowered cultivars of this shrubby perennial. It is easily propagated from cuttings in early

LEFT: Showy gloxina shows up well against a background of maidenhair fern; both are tender.

BELOW: The vibrant gloxina 'Duke of York'.

spring and plants can be put into the garden or containers during summer. Plants should be cut hard back after flowering is finished and kept quite dry during winter. Fuchsias like partial sun in moist soil.

Geraniums see **Pelargoniums**

Gloxinia

A rhizomatous perennial with clusters of showy, trumpet-shaped flowers that are white-edged in shades of pink, mauve and purple. During winter it should be kept quite dry; fresh leaves begin to emerge from the winter dormancy in early spring to flower for Easter. Requires partial shade and moist soil.

ABOVE: Hippeastrum bulbs are favourite Christmas gifts.

BELOW: Gloxina mixed with African violets.

Hippeastrum

Bulbous plants with broad, strap-like leaves and huge, funnel-shaped flowers. The bulbs are often sold pre-packed as Christmas presents. The bulbs should be planted to only half their depth in well-drained soil. Put in partial shade until leaf buds appear, then move to full sun. Keep bulbs dry during the winter when they are dormant.

Jasminum sambac

This is the most highly perfumed of the tender jasmines and the one grown in many Italian gardens, with a strong perfume that fills the garden as the sun begins to set. Grow in full sun and in rich, well-drained soil to do well.

Pelargoniums

Commonly called geraniums, these showy perennials come in a huge range of shapes, sizes, flower and foliage colour; some have scented leaves and are the ones on which I have based my collection. The varicoloured ornamental-leaf pelargoniums are also amusing to collect. Many of the zonal varieties have the largest, showiest flowers. Dead-head often to encourage continuous flowering. Cut the plants back by at least half their size to overwinter; keep on the dry side since they do not respond well to humid conditions. Grow in sun in well-drained soil.

Roses

Unless you live in the most intemperate climate, there are only a few roses that you will be able to grow with any success under glass. The gorgeous 'Maréchal Niel' is one; it has

ABOVE: Hippeastrum.

BELOW: Scented-leaf geraniums are good plants to begin with.

ABOVE: The extravagant flowers of *Pelargonium grandiflorum* make a spectacular show in the greenhouse or garden.

wonderful tea-scented, apricot-tinted flowers and was a favourite in Victorian conservatory gardens. Rosa 'Devoniensis' is another treasure, with a strong perfume and large, billowy blooms the colour of ecru lace. Roses should be rooted into the soil floor of a greenhouse or else given a deep pot, filled with rich, well-drained soil and then fed regularly. Full sun suits them well.

Saintpaulia

Most commonly known as African violets, these evergreen plants form rosettes of hairy leaves supporting clusters of single or double flowers in white and shades of pink, purple and blue; some have lovely bi-coloured

flowers, ruffled petals or semi-double blooms. This is a good plant to form a collection. The plants do best in partial shade, a humid atmosphere and rich, moist soil. Minimum winter temperatures of 15°C/59°F.

ABOVE: *Pelargonium zonale.*

BELOW: African violet 'Fusspot'.

Schlumbergera bridgesii

This plant is more easily recognised as the Christmas cactus. It makes clusters of segmented leaves, the tips of which burst into richly coloured magenta and red flowers; there are white and pink flowered forms also. Likes partial shade and well-drained soil.

INDEX

(References to photographs are indicated by *italics*.)

Picture Acknowledgments

The work of the following photographers has been used:
David Askham: 13(t), 14; **Roy Asser**: 48(t); **Lynne Brotchie**: 59(t); **Brian Carter**: 12, 45(t), 51, 60(t); **Chris Burrows**: 58(b); **Bob Challinor**: 6, 18, 19, 39, 54(b); **Densey Clyne**: 50, 57(b), 59(b); **Geoff Dann**: 13(b); **Robert Estall**: 15; **Vaughan Fleming**: 41(t), 53; **Nigel Francis**: 41(b); **John Glover**: i, 31, 48(b), 52(b), 54(t), 56(t)(b), 60(b); **Sunniva Harte**: 47; **Marijke Heuff**: 23; **Neil Holmes**: 32, 43(b), 55, 57(t), 62(b); **Michael Howes**: 11, 20(t), 21, 22, 24(t), 25, 26, 28(b), 29(b), 33(b), 35, 27, 40(t), 49(t); **Ann Kelley**: 52(t); **Lamontagne**: 61; **Jane Legate**: 20(b), 28(t), 29(t); **Mayer/Le Scanff**: 10, 17, 30, 38, jacket; **Zara McCalmont**: 7, 16, 46; **Jerry Pavia**: 8; **Howard Rice**: 62(t); **Stephen Robson**: 9; **Gary Rogers**, ii; **Lorna Rose**: 58(t); **JS Sira**: 40(b), 42(t)(b), 44, 45(b); **Ron Sutherland**: 27; **Juliette Wade**: 34, 49(b); **Mel Watson**: 24(b), 43(t); **Paul Windsor**: 36; **Steven Wooster**: 33(t).

The following gardens were photographed:
Herworth House, England: 16; **Cheveley, Newmarket, England**: 7, 46; **Admington House, Warwickshire, England**: 6; **Hampton Court Flower Show '91, England**: 9; **Pinewood House, England**: 12; **Lackham College, England**: 13(t); **Pershore Horticultural College, Chelsea Flower Show 1988, London, England**: 13(b); **St. Jean De Beauregard**: 17; **106 Ruxley Land, England**: 20(b).

The following shops supplied plants:
Collins & Browns Conservatory plants: 33(t).